Endorsements for the Church Questions Series

"Christians are pressed by very real questions. How does Scripture structure a church, order worship, organize ministry, and define biblical leadership? Those are just examples of the questions that are answered clearly, carefully, and winsomely in this new series from 9Marks. I am so thankful for this ministry and for its incredibly healthy and hopeful influence in so many faithful churches. I eagerly commend this series."

R. Albert Mohler Jr., President, The Southern Baptist Theological Seminary

"Sincere questions deserve thoughtful answers. If you're not sure where to start in answering these questions, let this series serve as a diving board into the pool. These mini-books are winsomely to-the-point and great to read together with one friend or one hundred friends."

Gloria Furman, author, *Missional Motherhood* and *The Pastor's Wife*

"As a pastor, I get asked lots of questions. I'm approached by unbelievers seeking to understand the gospel, new believers unsure about next steps, and maturing believers wanting help answering questions from their Christian family, friends, neighbors, or coworkers. It's in these moments that I wish I had a book to give them that was brief, answered their questions, and pointed them in the right direction for further study. Church Questions is a series that provides just that. Each booklet tackles one question in a biblical, brief, and practical manner. The series may be called Church Questions, but it could be called 'Church Answers.' I intend to pick these up by the dozens and give them away regularly. You should too."

Juan R. Sanchez, Senior Pastor, High Pointe Baptist Church, Austin, Texas

What Should
I Do Now That
I'm a Christian?

Church Questions

What Should
I Do Now That
I'm a Christian?

Sam Emadi

WHEATON, ILLINOIS

Trade paperback ISBN: 978-1-4335-6810-7
ePub ISBN: 978-1-4335-6813-8
PDF ISBN: 978-1-4335-6811-4
Mobipocket ISBN: 978-1-4335-6812-1

Library of Congress Cataloging-in-Publication Data

Names: Emadi, Sam, author.
Title: What should I do now that I'm a Christian? / Sam Emadi.
Description: Wheaton : Crossway, 2020. | Series: Church questions
Identifiers: LCCN 2019025539 (print) | LCCN 2019025540 (ebook) | ISBN 9781433568107 (trade paperback) | ISBN 9781433568114 (pdf) | ISBN 9781433568121 (mobi) | ISBN 9781433568138 (epub)
Subjects: LCSH: Christian life.
Classification: LCC BV4501.3 .E4592 2020 (print) | LCC BV4501.3 (ebook) | DDC 248.4—dc23
LC record available at https://lccn.loc.gov/2019025539
LC ebook record available at https://lccn.loc.gov/2019025540

Crossway is a publishing ministry of Good News Publishers.

BP		29	28	27	26	25	24	23	22	21	20
15	14	13	12	11	10	9	8	7	6	5	4	3	2	1

But you are a chosen race, a royal priesthood, a holy nation, a people for his own possession, that you may proclaim the excellencies of him who called you out of darkness into his marvelous light. Once you were not a people, but now you are God's people; once you had not received mercy, but now you have received mercy.

1 Peter 2:9–10

Born with a painful and debilitating disability, my friend Derek spent much of his early life in constant pain and barely able to walk. In his late teens, he turned to drugs as a way of coping with the pressures of his disability and as a way of gaining influence and approval among his friends.

Derek sold and used drugs for years. Whatever money he made selling drugs, he used to buy more, and he even stole from his family to fund his addiction. And yet, amid all of this, Derek maintained that he was a good person. After all, he was loyal to his friends and didn't do what he considered "the worst" drugs.

But Derek's life unalterably changed when he began visiting church with a friend. He heard the gospel for the first time, and he realized that he was a sinner under God's just condemnation. Listening to sermon after sermon, Derek discovered that God sent his Son, Jesus, to rescue sinners from his own wrath. And one day it all clicked: Derek knew he needed forgiveness. He knew he needed what only Jesus's cross and resurrection could provide. So he repented of his sin, believed in Jesus, and committed to following Christ as his Lord.

My church is full of people with stories just like Derek's. James enslaved himself to pornography for nearly a decade until a friend invited him to church where he believed the gospel. Parker grew up in a Christian home and trusted Christ at age twelve after studying the Bible with his dad. Ann thought God loved her because she was "a good kid," until she attended a Bible conference where she realized that in light of God's holiness, her righteousness was like "a polluted garment" (Isa. 64:6). Brittany felt adrift and purposeless in life until she became a Christian at a work Bible study.

If you're reading this book, I assume that you identify with these stories of grace. At some point—perhaps even recently—you recognized your need to be forgiven of sin and freed from sin's reign over your life. You turned to the crucified and resurrected Christ for salvation, and you desire to follow him.

But what now?

What does it *mean* to follow Jesus? What do you need to know so you can follow Jesus *for the rest of your life*?

No two Christians are exactly alike. We differ from one another in age, ethnicity, income, marital status, vocation, and a variety of other ways. Thankfully, no matter where you've been and no matter what you're doing now, the Bible gives you, me, and everyone the blueprint for how to thrive as a disciple of Jesus.

Setting Our Expectations

One of the most important parts of any journey is having the right expectations. I once set out on a road trip that I expected to take three hours. After six hours in the car, my road rage took a turn for the worse. Of course, I'd happily taken road trips much longer than six hours in the past. But the problem this time was that I hadn't *expected* to be in the car for so long. Having the right expectations informs how we respond to our circumstances.

As we think about the Christian life, it's also important to have the right expectations. As a friend of mine often puts it, we must always remember that following Jesus is costly, but it's also worth it. Jesus himself warned that we must count the cost of being his disciple (Luke 14:25–33). Being a Christian requires denying ourselves, taking up our crosses, and following Christ—wherever he may lead (Luke 9:23). Paul warned that "all who desire to live a godly life in Christ Jesus will be persecuted" (2 Tim. 3:12). Peter taught that we should "not be surprised" by the "fiery trials" we will encounter in this life (1 Pet. 4:12). The gospel promises us salvation from God's wrath and freedom from sin; it doesn't ever promise an easy life.

In this life we'll continue to sin, we'll stumble, and we'll fall. Often unintentionally, we'll hurt those we love. Even as we see victory over sin and growth in personal holiness, our lives will be characterized by repentance—a constant turning from sin to the grace of God found in Jesus Christ. Following Jesus is costly.

But following Jesus is also worth it. Yes, the cost of discipleship is high, but those costs pale in comparison to the joy of knowing God and being forgiven of all our sins. Paul said, "For this light momentary affliction is preparing for us an eternal weight of glory beyond all comparison" (2 Cor. 4:17). As we follow Christ, we should expect to grow in holiness. We should expect God's grace to make us more like Jesus (Rom. 8:28–29; Gal. 5:16–17). We'll face trials, sin, and temptation, but we'll also learn to confess to God and say along with the psalmist: "You make known to me the path of life; in your presence there is fullness of joy; at your right hand are pleasures forevermore" (Ps. 16:11).

What Should I Do Now That I'm a Christian?

With that foundation in place, let's lay out some specific things you should do now that you're a Christian. No matter your circumstances, this roadmap will help you thrive as a disciple of Jesus. These spiritually healthy practices aren't what make you (or keep you) a Christian, but they are practices that God has given us to help us grow in following our Lord with joy.

1) Get Baptized

If you've recently become a Christian, the first thing you should do is get baptized. Why? Because baptism is how Jesus commanded Christians to publicly profess their faith in him. When Jesus commissioned the church to make disciples, he told them to mark out those disciples with the act of baptism (Matt. 28:19). Jesus's instructions are quite clear: believe the gospel; get baptized.

The book of Acts gives us many examples of people coming to faith in Jesus and then publicly declaring that faith in baptism. Consider this account in Acts 2. We'll pick up the story just after Peter finished preaching an evangelistic sermon to a crowd of unbelievers.

> Now when [the crowd] heard [Peter's sermon] they were cut to the heart, and said to Peter and the rest of the apostles, "Brothers, what shall we do?" And Peter said to them, "Repent and be baptized every one of you in the name of Jesus Christ for the forgiveness of your sins, and you will receive the gift of the Holy Spirit. . . . So those who received his word were baptized, and there were added that day about three thousand souls. (Acts 2:37–38, 41)

"Repent and be baptized." In Scripture, the latter always follows the former.

When we repent of our sins, we turn to Christ and give him control over our lives. He calls the shots and sets the agenda. We submit to his instructions and follow him as Lord. Baptism manifests this commitment. When we're baptized, we make a public profession of our faith in Christ. We're saying to the world, "I belong to Jesus." As a friend of mine says, when we're baptized, we put on the "Team Jesus" jersey.[1] We belong to him.

Additionally, baptism symbolizes your new life in Christ. Going under the water depicts your dying with Christ. Emerging from the water depicts your resurrection from spiritual death, your new life in Christ (Rom. 6:3–4; Col. 2:11–12).

Finally, baptism is how a church affirms your profession of faith and receives you into membership. We'll think more about the importance of the local church in the following sections. For now, let's simply notice that Jesus gave the ordinance of baptism to the church (Matt. 28:18–20). The Bible records that the early church brought people into membership by baptizing them after they'd shown evidence of genuine repentance (Acts 2:41). When we follow Christ in baptism, we're declaring our allegiance to Jesus, and at the same time the church is affirming that our allegiance is genuine—giving their stamp of approval to our understanding of the gospel.

What should you do now that you're a Christian? Find a faithful, gospel-preaching, Bible-loving church—and pursue baptism.

2) Join a Local Church

In Christ, God has forgiven us of our sins and received us as sons and daughters. He's not only acquitted us in his courtroom, he's invited us to his family dinner table. Through Christ, we know God as our Father—we have a personal relationship with God.

But we shouldn't confuse a *personal* relationship with a *private* relationship. Yes, through Christ we know God personally, but God never intended for us to follow him on our own, privately, as lone ranger Christians. God saves us *into* a community, and he designed our relationship with him to include fellow brothers and sisters who are walking the same path of obedience. Being reconciled to God means being reconciled to his people (Eph. 2:11–12; 1 Pet. 2:10).

The New Testament is filled with "one another" passages precisely because God intends for us to be in community with other Christians. Consider how frequently Scripture commands us to serve and love other believers.

- A new commandment I give to you, that you love *one another*: just as I have loved you, you also are to love *one another*. By this all people will know that you are my disciples, if you have love for *one another*. (John 13:34–35)
- Love *one another* with brotherly affection. Outdo *one another* in showing honor. . . . Live in harmony with *one another*. (Rom. 12:10, 16)
- Only do not use your freedom as an opportunity for the flesh, but through love serve *one another*. (Gal. 5:13)
- Be kind to *one another*, tenderhearted, forgiving one another, as God in Christ forgave you. (Eph. 4:32)
- Put on then, as God's chosen ones, holy and beloved, compassionate hearts, kindness, humility, meekness, and patience, bearing with *one another* and, if one has a complaint against

another, forgiving *each other*; as the Lord has forgiven you, so you also must forgive. . . . Let the word of Christ dwell in you richly, teaching and admonishing *one another* in all wisdom, singing psalms and hymns and spiritual songs, with thankfulness in your hearts to God. (Col. 3:12–13, 16)

- Therefore encourage *one another* and build *one another* up, just as you are doing. (1 Thess. 5:11)
- And let us consider how to stir up *one another* to love and good works. (Heb. 10:24)

That's only a fraction of Scripture's "one another" passages.

The Christian life isn't a call to isolated devotion, like a monk in a cave. Instead, the heart of Christian obedience is a life of love for other believers in a local church fueled by faith in Christ—or as Paul writes, "faith working through love" (Gal. 5:6).

By joining a church, you commit yourself to doing the type of "one another" work mentioned in the list above. By joining a church, you're essentially saying, "I want to follow Jesus's commands, and I'm committing to do that with *these* people."

It's quite easy to get excited about the *idea* of loving and serving others, but *actually* loving others is something altogether more challenging. After all, our brothers and sisters in Christ, like you and I, are sinners. They will step on our toes. They will hurt us, intentionally and unintentionally. Fellow church members will frustrate us, even wound us—and we will do the same to them.

Nevertheless, the Bible doesn't qualify its commands: "Love your neighbor . . . when it's easy." No, Scripture continually points us back to the local church as the place where we can grow into Christlikeness. In a local church, we learn to forgive others (Eph. 4:32), to carry others' burdens (Gal. 6:2), and to bear with one another in love (Eph. 4:2). As we obey Christ's command to love others as he has loved us, the local church showcases to the world the love of Christ and the glory of the gospel (John 13:34–35).

In fact, let me make an even more radical claim.

Joining a local church isn't simply one aspect of your Christian life. *The local church is the primary context where you live out your Christian discipleship.* Consider it this way: Have you ever gone to a Christian bookstore and noticed one section of the store marked "the church" and another section marked "the Christian life"? Those two sections should really be one and the same. The Christian life orbits around the church. We worship God, love others, serve our brothers and sisters, suffer, study the Bible, pray, give, grieve, and evangelize—all in the context of a local church. Remember, your conversion made you part of God's family, and living as a Christian means living like a family member—embracing God as Father means embracing other redeemed sinners as brothers and sisters.

In fact, every other point in this book is really just an explanation of what it looks like to faithfully live the Christian life in a local church.

What should you do now that you're a Christian? Join a local church and learn to follow Jesus among his people.

3) Attend Your Church Regularly

Dinner is an important time for my family. Every morning, my family scatters. My wife runs errands, the kids engage in school or sports programs, and I head to work always a little later than anticipated. But each evening we gather again around the dinner table. My kids tell me about their activities. My wife updates me about her day. We share stories. We laugh. We learn more about each other and about ourselves as a family. By gathering together each night, we reinforce our commitment to and love for one another. Regularly gathering reinforces that we are family, not just strangers sharing a meal.

The same principle applies to church life. By regularly gathering, we submit ourselves to God's preached word every week, and we show we're committed to loving *this* group of people.

By regularly gathering, we get to know and be known by our fellow church members.

More than that, the Bible explicitly commands regular church attendance:

> And let us consider how to stir up one another to love and good works, not neglecting to meet together, as is the habit of some, but encouraging one another, and all the more as you see the Day drawing near. (Heb. 10:24–25)

Notice two things in this passage. First, the author of Hebrews condemns "neglecting to meet together." Part of Christian obedience, then, is regular church attendance. We can't claim to love God if we only occasionally gather with his people to worship him and hear from his word.

Second, notice that the opposite of "neglecting to meet together" isn't "meeting together." Instead, it's "encouraging one another." When we fail to gather with our local church, we're robbing our brothers and sisters of encouragement.

We're failing to "stir up one another to love and good works." So we encourage others *by* gathering with them.

You might feel as though you don't do anything on Sundays, apart from just "showing up." But even in this mere ministry of regular attendance, other saints are encouraged as they see and hear you singing the same songs, confessing the same faith, submitting to the same Scriptures, and trusting the same Savior. Christians should never underestimate the lasting influence their regular presence has on the spiritual good of other believers.

By regularly attending your local church, you'll also fulfill Jesus's command to participate in the Lord's Supper (Luke 22:19).[2] When we celebrate the Lord's Supper, we commemorate the death of Christ and renew our ultimate hope in his return (1 Cor. 11:26). In the Lord's Supper, we also reaffirm our commitment to the members of our local church and show our unity in the gospel (1 Cor. 10:17). The Lord's Supper is the family meal for God's people, the table where we confess our hope in Christ and love for one another—together.

What should you do now that you're a Christian? Attend your church regularly.

4) Study the Bible

For months, my daughter endured an irritating skin rash. Despite our best efforts, my wife and I couldn't find a way to get rid of it. After several lotions, creams, and trips to the doctor, we were stumped. Then one day, the light bulb came on. What if it was related to food? By experimenting with my daughter's diet, we isolated the specific foods that caused her skin to break out. Her skin cleared up almost immediately. With the right nutrition, my little girl was healthy again!

Our spiritual health is also a matter of getting the right nutrition. We nourish our souls and grow into maturity by "Bible intake"—reading, hearing, meditating on, and studying Scripture. If we feed our minds with lies, sin, or worldly wisdom, then our spiritual health and relationship with God will suffer.

Jesus and the apostles regularly spoke of Scripture as "spiritual food." For instance, Jesus said that we don't live by physical bread alone but by "every word that comes from the mouth of God" (Matt. 4:4). The apostle Peter, referring to Scripture, encourages us to desire "pure spiritual milk" so that we "grow up" to spiritual maturity (1 Pet. 2:2).

Simply put, the Bible is our spiritual food. If we don't regularly take in Scripture, then we'll be spiritually malnourished, unhealthy, and susceptible to sin.

The reason we need to regularly take in Scripture is because it's unlike any other book. The Bible is the very word of God. When Scripture speaks, God speaks. In fact, the apostle Paul taught not only that the Bible is inspired by God, but it is also able to equip us for "every good work" (2 Tim. 3:16–17). Do you want to know how to follow Christ in *every* area of life? Open up your Bible.

The most frequent way Christians take in Scripture is through personal Bible reading. By reading Scripture each day, we remind ourselves of the gospel and fill our minds with biblical truth. As one pastor has said, don't approach Scripture like antibiotics, only ingesting it in a crisis, but like a daily vitamin, providing spiritual nutrients for daily life.

One good way to regularly read Scripture is to commit to a Bible-reading plan. (I've listed a few at the end of this book.) As the old adage goes, people don't plan to fail, they fail to plan. Committing to a reading plan can help you know what to read each day and ensures that you're exposed to all of Scripture—not just reading the same few books over and over.

But let me warn you: even with a reading plan, regular Bible reading is a challenge. You'll miss days, even weeks. The tyranny of the urgent will lure you away from Scripture, and indwelling sin and Satan will seek to keep you from God's word. But even in those moments, remember that anything worth doing is still worth doing poorly. So don't let missed days (or weeks or months) keep you from coming back to Scripture and re-engaging with God's word.

Nourish your soul with God's word, but remember a good meal should never be enjoyed alone. I hate eating alone—especially in a restaurant. My thoughts tend to run wild: *What should I look at? Is it sad if I just stare at my food? Does it look like I'm crying in my plate? I can't look up; people will think I'm staring at them . . . and that looks creepy. Do people here think I don't have any friends? Maybe they think I'm a spy. No, nobody thinks I'm a spy. People just think I don't have any friends. Should I invite the waiter to sit down? Why didn't I bring a book!*

Almost every culture on the planet makes meals the center of hospitality and fellowship. Why? Because meals are meant to be enjoyed with others. With forks in our hands (rather than smartphones), we look across the table and say, "Isn't this good!" We enhance our enjoyment of a meal by enjoying it *with* others.

The same principle applies with studying Scripture. We're meant to feast on God's word with other redeemed sinners. Remember what I said earlier about the centrality of the local church in the Christian life? Even with Bible intake, we're not meant to go it alone. In the local church, we hear God's word explained and applied. The church does this formally through its preaching and teaching ministry, and informally through the relationships believers build with one another.

In the local church, God's people "devote themselves to the apostles' teaching" (Acts 2:42). Pastors and elders, men trained to teach the Bible (1 Tim. 3:2), give their lives to helping the congregation rightly understand and apply Scripture (2 Tim. 4:2). Fellow church members speak "the truth in love" to one another so that they "grow up" spiritually and look more like Christ (Eph. 4:15).

The more fully we integrate into the life of a local church, the more opportunities we'll have to receive God's word. Instead of only reading God's word for ourselves, we get to hear God's word echo from person to person as we speak God's word to one another. Just consider how this worked for my friends Jonathan and Stephanie. Before Jonathan and

Stephanie joined a church, their interaction with Scripture was minimal. Jonathan tried to read Scripture 15 minutes each morning but only hit that mark about four days a week. With small kids at home, Stephanie felt overwhelmed by parenting and rarely read the Bible—a habit that left her feeling constantly guilty.

Eventually, Jonathan and Stephanie joined a church and found that their knowledge of the Bible began to blossom. They started attending Sunday school and the Sunday sermon. This act alone dramatically increased the amount of regular exposure they had to God's word. Additionally, the Sunday school classes helped them understand the Bible's big picture, teaching them how to study the Bible more effectively for themselves.

In fact, the Sunday sermon became something of a focal point for Bible intake; it shaped their entire week. Jonathan and Stephanie began to spend 3–5 minutes each night before bed reading over the Scripture passage the pastor planned to preach the next Sunday to prepare their hearts for the message. Additionally, the couple joined a church small group that met, in part, to discuss how to apply the sermon text to their lives.

As they began to build more friendships at church, Jonathan found that he worked at the same company as another church member. They began meeting for lunch every Wednesday—just to discuss Ephesians and to pray. Similarly, Stephanie joined a mom's Bible study on Tuesday mornings.

More than that, Jonathan and Stephanie's friends at church seemed to constantly expose them to the Bible in new ways. At a cookout, a friend relayed, "I got some real help with my parenting reading Philippians this week. Here's what I saw . . ." Another friend confided, "I was having a rough time in my marriage, but the Lord helped me see how I wasn't following this command in 1 Corinthians . . ." Later in the week, over dinner, a couple said, "We've been so encouraged by how the church models this passage in 1 Timothy . . ." Jonathan and Stephanie noticed how even ordinary conversations about a wide variety of topics were peppered with bits of Scripture. The Bible surrounded them, echoing in every corner of their lives and relationships. The local church was an echo chamber for Scripture.

Bible intake—both private and church-wide—fuels our faith in the gospel and gives us strength to follow Jesus and fight sin.

So, what should you do now that you're a Christian? Study the Bible for yourself and with others in your local church.

5) Pray Regularly

I'm amazed by the Bible. The fact that God would reveal himself to us and speak to us in Scripture is astounding. But what's perhaps equally astounding is that God allows us to speak back to him. Because we've been redeemed by Christ, God invites us to come before him and express our adoration, praise, and thanksgiving—as well as our concerns, anxieties, frustrations, and tears. Christ stands as our righteousness and advocate before the

Father, so that we can now "with confidence draw near to the throne of grace, that we may receive mercy and find grace to help in time of need" (Heb. 4:16).

In other words, Christians pray.

The New Testament regularly invites us to pray. Jesus expects his people to pray and even gives them a template for prayer (Matt. 6:5–13). Paul encourages Christians to pray "at all times" (Eph. 6:18) and even commands that we pray "without ceasing" (1 Thess. 5:17). Obviously, Paul's not suggesting Christians engage in an endless personal devotion. Rather, the posture of every Christian's heart should be one of prayer. Our reflex to life ought to be praying to God. As one pastor said, for the Christian, prayer ought to be like breathing.[3]

But just like Bible intake, praying regularly is hard work. So how do we develop the discipline of a healthy prayer life?

First, pray regularly in private. Along with your Bible reading, spend some time in prayer. How do you choose what to pray about each day? Naturally, we'll gravitate toward what's important to us: our families, our health, or difficult circumstances. But that still leaves us wondering, *How* should we pray for our children? *How* should we pray for our spouse? *How* should we pray for our circumstances?

The best way to pray is to let the Bible inform your prayer life. As you read Scripture, respond to the truth of God's word with prayer. For example:

- As you read passages about God's character, praise God for who he is. Ask that others would also praise God for these same reasons.
- As you read about God's acts, thank God for his physical and spiritual provision. Ask that others would recognize God's provision in their lives and respond with thankfulness.
- As you read about Christ, praise God for the many blessings of salvation he has provided for you. Ask him to help you trust more fully in the gospel. Pray the same for other believers. Pray that the lost people in your life would be saved, and that God would give you opportunities to share the gospel with them.

- As you read about God's promises, ask God to help you believe those promises and walk in light of them. Pray the same for others.
- As you read God's laws and commands, confess the ways you've failed and ask for help to keep them in the future.
- Finally, apply these truths to your circumstances and make specific requests of God in light of them.

For more help on how Scripture can govern your prayer life, pick up Don Whitney's excellent little book *Praying the Bible*.[4]

Second, pray with other believers in your local church. At this point, you shouldn't be surprised to learn that the local church plays a central role in helping us develop a healthy prayer life.

Scripture regularly highlights prayer as a central aspect of local church life. In Acts 2:42, the early church devotes itself to "the apostles' teaching and the fellowship, to the breaking of bread and the *prayers*." Throughout Acts we find local churches, church leaders, or church members praying together (4:23–31; 6:1–6;

8:14–15; 12:1–5; 13:1–3; 20:36). Think of the local church as a teaching hospital for prayer. When we gather with God's people, we both pray and learn the discipline of prayer.

As you invest in the life of your local church, find ways to participate in corporate prayer and to pray with others. Here are just a few ways the local church gives shape to our prayer life:

- Consider carefully the corporate prayers on Sunday morning and let them influence your prayers throughout the week. The prayers of your whole congregation should reflect the content of your own prayers as well.
- Learn from corporate prayer how to confess sin, praise God, offer thanks, and make requests.
- If your church has a membership directory, pray through it systematically. Pick a few people every day and pray for them. Even if you don't know them, you can pray that God would keep them from sin and strengthen their faith in the gospel.

- If your church has a weekly prayer meeting, regularly attend it. Don't miss out on the opportunity to watch God visibly answer the public prayers of his people.
- Pay attention to the items your pastor regularly prays for or asks others to pray for. For instance, if your pastor regularly asks for people to pray for faithful preaching in the church, more consistent hospitality, or faithfulness and fruitfulness in evangelism, then make those same concerns a part of your prayer life.
- Make it a habit to pray with other members, even if only for a few minutes over coffee.

What should you do now that you're a Christian? Spend time in prayer by yourself, with your church, and with other believers.

6) Be Discipled by Others

I love playing the handyman around my house, though I admit I'm not great at actually fixing anything. Most of the time, I quickly run right past the boundaries of my competence. But what I lack in competence, I make up for in shameless pleas for help. I may not know how to fix a dishwasher, but I know whom to call for help, and by God's grace, I have friends who are willing to come to my aid. The glorious thing about these relationships is how much I learn from friends who are more capable than I am. I used to need help with every minor home repair. But after learning from others, I can capably tackle basic issues.

Just like I needed friends to teach me basic home repair, we need friends who will teach us how to follow Jesus. This is especially true for brand-new Christians, but it is important for Christians of all stages. We need discipling—relationships that teach us how to follow Jesus.

Discipling relationships are crucial to the Christian life. Hopefully, your local church has more seasoned brothers and sisters in the faith who have walked the path of obedience and learned lessons they can pass on to you. Through our relationships with them, we learn how to walk with God.

Jesus and the apostles modeled discipling relationships for us. Jesus spent intentional time with his disciples, teaching them how to follow him. Some of this happened through formal teaching but much of it was informal as they simply lived life together (John 13). Jesus even seemed to have a particularly close discipling relationship with Peter, James, and John. Likewise, Paul personally invested in his protégé Timothy and encouraged him to disciple others just as Paul discipled him (2 Tim. 2:2).

If we follow the pattern of Jesus and the apostles, we'll pursue discipling relationships in our local church. We will disciple and be discipled.

But how do we pursue discipling relationships?

The best way is to simply start investing in people in your local church. Make a habit of inviting others over to your home for meals. Have lunch with other believers. It doesn't matter what you do—go bowling together if you prefer—just make it a priority to get together.

Another practical step might be to prioritize showing up early and staying late at church services so that you can spend time talking to other members. I've always made it a goal to talk to one person after our Sunday morning service I didn't know well and to have a meaningful conversation with a close friend after our Sunday evening service. As you pursue others in your church, you'll find that opportunities for discipling relationships will emerge naturally and organically.

Christian friendships are among the sweetest gifts God gives his people. Don't just view your church as a place where you hear preaching. Instead, invest in the people there. Learn to follow Jesus through rich friendships with other believers, and then teach others to do the same.

What should you do now that you're a Christian? Disciple and be discipled.

7) Give to the Church

In the Christian life, we advance the gospel by partnering with other brothers and sisters in our local church to move the gospel forward in the world. We can accomplish far more together for the kingdom of God than we can alone.

One of the primary ways we partner together is by giving financially to the church. The New Testament regularly *commands* and *commends* financial generosity for the sake of advancing the gospel (2 Cor. 9:7–15; 1 Tim. 6:17–19; Heb. 13:16). God explicitly *commands* that we give to the work of the ministry (Gal. 6:6) as an act of devotion and obedience to God. The Bible also regularly *commends* giving as one of the primary ways Christians advance the gospel. Early Christian churches sold possessions to ensure that no church members were in physical need (Acts 2:45; 4:34), cared for the needs of other local churches (2 Cor. 8:1–4), and paid their pastors and missionaries so they could advance the gospel by building healthy local churches (1 Tim. 5:17–18).

By giving financially to the church, we equip the church to care for its members, ensure that pastors can focus on the task of shepherding, and catalyze evangelism and missions both near and far. We should never think of just one person doing *this* ministry and another person doing *that* ministry. Instead, we *partner* in ministry with one another—sharing in one another's endeavors for the cause of Christ. And we do this in part by giving.

This language of ministry "partnership" comes from the apostle Paul. He commended the church in Philippi for "partnering" with him in his missionary endeavors by caring for his physical needs (Phil. 1:5; 4:14–19). As we give to the church, we become colaborers in all the ministries represented by the whole church. We become partners in gospel work—whether we're on the front line or in the supply line.

What should you do now that you're a Christian? Give financially to your local church.

8) Evangelize the Lost

Finally, in these last pages, let me encourage you to evangelize the lost. Evangelism means telling others the message of the gospel and inviting them to respond to Christ with faith and repentance. As recipients of God's grace, we have the privilege of representing Christ to others and encouraging them to believe the gospel.

Jesus commanded that we take the gospel to all nations (Matt. 28:18–20), and all Christians in the early church—not just the pastors—faithfully shared the gospel with those around them (Acts 8:1, 4). The mission of the church is to make disciples of the Lord Jesus. One way believers fulfill that mission is by faithfully speaking about Christ with friends, coworkers, family members, neighbors, taxi drivers, grocery-store clerks, and anyone else in their spheres of influence.

Evangelism is difficult. It requires patience, courage, and building intentional relationships with unbelievers. Ultimately, no magic formula makes evangelism "work." Our responsibility is simply to share the gospel as winsomely and as faithfully as possible and trust that as we plant the seed of the gospel, God will open the hearts of some to receive it (Acts 16:14).

Even as we seek to faithfully evangelize, we must remember that we're not alone in this work. Our local churches aid and fuel our evangelistic efforts. Our relationships in the local church showcase the love of Christ to the world

(John 13:35; 17:20–21), and the care members have for one another is often a means the Lord uses to make people more receptive to the gospel. In our local churches, we help one another rightly understand and articulate the gospel, we train each other to share the gospel well, we hold one another accountable to evangelize, we evangelize together, and we pray for one another's evangelistic efforts. As we labor to be faithful in evangelism, we must remember that Jesus never meant for us to go it alone. The local church is a community of evangelists that encourages and helps one another in their evangelistic efforts.

What should you do now that you're a Christian? Evangelize the lost.

Persevering to the End

Following Jesus is costly, but it's worth it. As we seek to follow after Jesus, we should always remember that we're never called to go it alone. Jesus always gives us his church, and he always promises us his presence (Matt. 28:20).

As you follow Christ in these ways, never lose sight of the fact that the grace of God and the promises of the gospel are ultimately what sustain your faith and obedience to God. We rest ultimately on this promise: "He who began a good work in you will bring it to completion at the day of Jesus Christ" (Phil. 1:6).

Recommended Resources

Bible-Reading Plans

The M'Cheyne Reading Plan is available online at https://www.mcheyne.info/calendar.pdf.

The *Discipleship Journal* Bible Reading Plan is available online at https://www.navigators.org/wp-content/uploads/2017/04/Discipleship-Journal-Bible-Reading-Plan-9781617479083.pdf.

The Two-Year Bible Reading Plan is available online at https://www.thegospelcoalition.org/article/two-year-bible-reading-plan/.

The Bible Reading Plan for Shirkers and Slackers is available online at https://ransomfellowship.org/wp-content/uploads/2017/03

/Bible-Reading-Program-for-Shirkers-and
-Slackers.pdf.

More Books on the Christian Life

Thabiti Anyabwile, *What Is a Healthy Church Member?* (Wheaton, IL: Crossway, 2008).

Mark Dever, *The Gospel and Personal Evangelism* (Wheaton, IL: Crossway, 2017).

Bobby Jamieson, *Understanding Baptism* (Wheaton, IL: Crossway, 2016).

Jonathan Leeman, *Church Membership: How the World Knows Who Represents Jesus* (Wheaton, IL: Crossway, 2012).

J. I. Packer, *Knowing God* (Downers Grove, IL: InterVarsity Press, 1973).

Donald S. Whitney, *Praying the Bible* (Wheaton, IL: Crossway, 2015).

Donald S. Whitney, *Spiritual Disciplines for the Christian Life* (Colorado Springs, CO: NavPress, 2014).

Donald S. Whitney, *Spiritual Disciplines within the Church: Participating Fully in the Body of Christ* (Chicago, IL: Moody, 1996).

Notes

1. Bobby Jamieson, *Going Public: Why Baptism Is Required for Church Membership* (Nashville, TN: B&H Academic, 2015), 99, 227.
2. The Lord's Supper is also sometimes called "communion."
3. John Onwuchekwa, *Prayer: How Praying Together Shapes the Church* (Wheaton, IL: Crossway, 2018), 17.
4. Donald S. Whitney, *Praying the Bible* (Wheaton, IL: Crossway, 2015).

Scripture Index

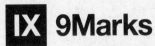

IX 9Marks

Building Healthy Churches

9Marks exists to equip church leaders with a biblical vision and practical resources for displaying God's glory to the nations through healthy churches.

To that end, we want to see churches characterized by these nine marks of health:

1. Expositional Preaching
2. Biblical Theology
3. A Biblical Understanding of the Gospel
4. A Biblical Understanding of Conversion
5. A Biblical Understanding of Evangelism
6. Biblical Church Membership
7. Biblical Chuch Discipline
8. Biblical Discipleship
9. Biblical Church Leadership

Find all our Crossway titles and other resources at 9Marks.org.

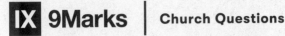

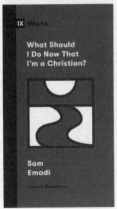